T0142529

Art of the Job Interview

MICHAEL CAVICANTE

authorHOUSE®

AuthorHouse™
1663 Liberty Drive
Bloomington, IN 47403
www.authorhouse.com
Phone: 833-262-8899

Published by AuthorHouse 09/03/2020

ISBN: 978-1-7283-7150-4 (sc)
ISBN: 978-1-7283-7372-0 (e)

PREFACE

Hello Job Applicants –

My name is Michael Cavicante, author also of "A Father's Double Life", which is an autobiography of my childhood. If you haven't read it, I would hope that you would, especially, if you or someone you know have been a victim of child/sexual abuse. It could help the healing process of such a traumatic experience.

After going through such a childhood, I was determined to make something of myself, and therefore had the will to do so, and have earned a six-digit income since the age of thirty-four (I am now fifty-four years of age).

Through my years of employment, most of which, in a supervisory capacity, and therefore have interviewed hundreds of applicants over the last 22 years, but also myself, have been on a lot of interviews. Fourteen to be exact, and have been offered the position on thirteen of those fourteen interviews, which includes being hired as a Branch Manager of a bank, but without a college degree or any prior banking experience. The latter being a feat which still holds most people in awe when I tell them about it.

And here is the thing. I have never read a book on how to interview, but yet, I have gotten the position on virtually every interview I have ever been on.

I guess you might say, "WOW!! That's a lot of interviews. He must have had a lot of jobs." … No, not true at all. Most of those jobs I declined either for pay, or other reasons. Some I went on just for the challenge of seeing if I could get the job or not, and then some, just for practice to keep my interviewing skills up.

As to what motivated me to write this book; well let's just say that based on what I have experienced when interviewing prospects, I wanted to help them (you).

I kept it short, because I want you to read it in its entirety, and not pick and choose what you want to read.

Everything I have included is important, and needs to be read.

Before we get into the art of the interview, there are some things that first must be addressed.

I often hear people say, "They can't discriminate and not hire me because of my tattoos, or piercings, or hair dyed purple or pink, excessive jewelry, etc."

And I must say, how fucking stupid is that comment?!!!!!

Pardon my French, and I am not one to use profanity, but I just had to in this case.

The fact of the matter is, if you don't get the job, you never know why. It is never disclosed to you, the interviewee. All you ever know is, that they moved on from you, and you were not offered the position. That's it!! You never know why you didn't get hired.

I personally have turned away many applicants simply based on their appearance. It's nothing personal. It's business.

So, for those of you who have aspirations of working in corporate America in white collar positions, you may think twice before tattooing your face, your neck, your wrists, your fingers, your ears, or anywhere tattoos can easily be seen.

Fact is, if you're going to be working on the front lines with that company's clients, they want you to look professional and well groomed, and not all tatted up.

If you are working behind the scenes in such positions as a cook, dishwasher, laborer, warehouse, auto mechanic, etc., then yes!! You will be able to get away with tattoos that are exposed, because you aren't open to the public.

Of course, if you have the talent of a singer such as Post Malone, then you are safe as well. But even as an actor, think about it. If you are all tatted up with markings all over your face, neck, etc. then your acting roles will be limited.

I don't have a problem with tattoos, but if you want to work in corporate America, on the front lines, keep the tattoos inconspicuous, and therefore, in places that normally are covered up with your clothes, and you will be safe from scrutiny.

Excessive piercings could also deter you from getting that job as well. You must understand that you want to be conservative during the interview, and not gaudy or outrageous.

Don't be putting huge holes in your ear lobes that resemble being part of some type of tribe. Avoid the piercings above the eye, and for guys, try to abstain from piercings all together.

Females, keep you earing count to no more than two per ear. A nose ring is fine, but needs to be subtle such as a stud. Avoid piercings on the lip and above the eyes. Limit your facial piercings to only your ears and nose. (Some employers may not even like the nose being pieced, but most will accept it.)

Now that we have gotten past the tattoos and the piercings, let's move on to how you should dress.

For both guys and girls, you want to wear neutral colors, and nothing too flashy or gaudy.

For both males and females, preferred colors are dark blue, black, or gray. Beiges and browns are okay, but try to ensure that these are all solid colors. Try to abstain from pinstripes (unless really thin and subtle).

Guys you want to wear a nice suit with a nice tie.

Girls, pant suits are perfectly fine. If you are wearing a skirt, make sure it is falls below the knee caps and please wear stockings/pantyhose. If you are well endowed up top, try not to expose your cleavage, and therefore wear a blouse that is going to cover you up.

If you are applying for a job in a male dominated field, the person interviewing you may think that you could be a distraction to the team, so you want to show that you're conservative and ladylike, and not a sexual harassment lawsuit waiting to happen.

Flat shoes are okay, but I recommend heels (no stilettoes), and no higher than two inches.

Lipstick is okay, but not too flashy. I would actually suggest no lipstick. Sometimes, lip gloss looks just as nice.

Your hair should be your natural color whether it be red, black, brown, etc, unless you want to dye it a common color. But stay away from off colors such as pink, red, purple, orange, yellow, etc. You want the person who is interviewing you to be paying attention to you, and not your weird hair color, or any other of the aforementioned items I have so far mentioned.

Guys and girls, also stay away from weird hairdos such as Mohawks, or shaving just one side of your head.

Stay away from wearing excessive jewelry on your hands and wrists. Girls and guys, limit rings on your fingers to one on each hand, and definitely no more than two per hand.

Same for your wrists. Limit your bracelets to just one if you must wear one.

Necklaces should be worn under your clothes; not on top of them.

Have you gotten my drift yet?

We want classy and conservative!! Not gaudy and extreme. We are looking for professionals.

It doesn't matter what you are applying for, look great when you go on your interview. It's a way of separating yourself apart from the rest of the candidates.

Now that you have an idea as to how to look and dress for your interview, let's now move into getting prepared for the interview.

So, whether you graduated from college or not, you've applied for several jobs and have some interviews lined up.

You get a call from the HR Department that the company you have applied for, would like to interview you.

There is nothing like the feeling that you get, when you get this notification. It is like one of the best feelings in the world. You're like WOW!! They are interested in me!! Yes, it is quite a rush.

And it shouldn't matter what you applied for, or what the position is. The fact that they called you should make you feel special.

Out of all the applicants, they chose you for the opportunity to fill the position.

So your interview is a week away; what do you do?

There is no particular order to get prepared for an interview, just as long as you are prepared when it's time.

If you are interviewing with a big company, you want to know certain things about that company, such as how many people they employ, who the CEO is, when the company was founded, what their stock price is, what mergers have they gone through, and what charities do they support to name a few.

Also, and I can't tell you how important this is. Do some investigative work in finding out what the starting salary or hourly wage is for the job you are applying for. This could be key in you landing the job, simply because, the question may arise as to what you expect your pay to be, and if you overshoot the starting pay for that position, you could very well lose out on the opportunity.

As you read in the preface, I landed a job as a Branch Manager for one of the biggest banks in the country, and without a college degree or any prior banking experience. I honestly feel that one of the reasons was because my pay expectations were significantly less, than what a Branch Manager should make.

When asked during my third interview, "Michael, so what are your pay expectations?" – My response was, $31900.00.

I had done my research and I knew that a Branch Manager at that time was making between $38,000 -$42,000.00, so I intentionally went significantly under that.

Why did I do that? Well obviously it was a tactic, but also, because I knew that I had no prior banking experience, nor a college degree, so how dare I suggest a salary as high as a Branch Manager that had one or both of these requirements.

By the way, the two requirements that I did meet, were, sales background, which I had from selling cars, and supervisory experience, which I had from the military. So I met two of the four requirements that they were looking for, which is what prompted me to apply for the position in the first place.

Anyway, after giving my response of $31,900, she says, "Okay Michael, that's fine. I need you to be in downtown Norfolk on Monday at HR to start orientation."

It actually took me a minute or so before it donned on me that I had gotten the job, when finally I asked, "I got the job?

"Yes Michael, you got the job."

"Really? I got the job?"

"Yes Michael, you got the job."

"Oh my gosh. I can't believe it!!"

"Well believe it."

"Oh my gosh!"

As I then went around to her side of the desk, picked her up and gave her a big hug, while saying, "Thank you so much!!"

Yes, it was one of the most amazing things that's ever happened to me.

I had already achieved a lot at this point in my life, but this by far was the most amazing feat in my opinion.

After being hired, I would go on to break sales records, be given three pay raises within the first fifteen months, and promoted to officer status. All of this before going back into the car business as a Finance Manager twenty one months later, at the age of thirty four, en route to a six digit income.

Due to a childhood of poverty, sexual abuse and foster homes, my grades suffered through high school and I graduated with a rank of seventy-eight out of eighty-two graduates.

It just goes to show you that you can do whatever you want in life if you put your mind to it.

Anyway, so you have done your research on the company and know everything that you think you should know about the company you are interviewing for.

You have picked out or shopped for a nice outfit, your nails are trimmed, you're clean shaven, and your hair is neatly trimmed, or have gotten that nice hairstyle. --- And oh, I forgot to tell you, stay away from perfume or cologne. The person who is interviewing you could have allergies, so abstain from wearing any fragrances. The pure smell of cleanliness should be enough.

Please know the location of where the interview is. If unfamiliar with the address or location, drive to the location of the interview the night before, so you know exactly where to go.

Yes, yes, I know. You have GPS on your phone. It doesn't matter. Drive to the location of the interview anyway so that you are familiar with where parking is, whether or not the parking free, or if there's any construction going on, or one way streets, etc. that you may have to navigate.

The key is being prepared for all aspects of the interview, and not just the interview itself.

On the day of the interview, leave in plenty of time to get there, not on time, but at least fifteen minutes early.

There is nothing that will turn the interviewer off more than being late for the interview.

While you are waiting, don't be slouched down in the chair or sofa. Exude good posture from the time you step into the office. Remove your gum before you enter the room. Do not be chewing gum!! You will be observed from the time you walk in the door.

So the receptionist has seated you and you're waiting, when the person interviewing you walks into the room with your file and calls your name.

I tell you today's young people, don't know how to say sir or ma'm anymore, but I got to tell you, it goes a long way. It shows that you were raised right, and shows respect.

When they walk out and call your name, you are to look them in the eyes with a big smile, and while standing, say, "Yes sir or ma'm." I'm Michael" and as they approach you, extend your right hand for a firm handshake, before they lead the way into their office.

The handshake is important. Guys, you don't want to bring the interviewer to their knees with a bone-crippling hand shake, and girls, you don't want the handshake to be too limp, or just use two or three fingers.

The handshake should be nice and firm, with the inner part of your thumb meeting theirs, and grabbing their whole hand firmly, for just a second or two – then release.

After being seated, keep your posture while sitting straight in the chair, but relaxed. Elbows can relax on armrests, with hands resting on the lap or knees.

Try not to be tense and just relax, and don't look so serious. Smile throughout the interview and be pleasant.

The interviewer may or may not confirm your name and the position you are applying for, and share some small talk in order to break the ice, to make you feel comfortable.

If you are a college graduate, they may ask you how you liked college, and what your long term goals are, etc.

You want to be candid and open, while expressing yourself freely.

Being tight and stiff is the wrong way to be. You should open up and talk to them as if you're talking to your best friend, and make them laugh.

If you can make the person interviewing you laugh, that will carry you a long way. The key is getting the person who is interviewing to like you. You will not get hired if they don't like you.

Don't be afraid to ask questions of the interviewer. If you see pictures on their desk or credenza of what seems to be their family, then compliment them, and ask who the people in the picture are.

People like to talk about themselves and family in particular, especially their kids. We love to gloat about our kids, so get them talking briefly about their family, kids, what they like to do etc.

The interview doesn't have to be all one-sided.

Find out how long they have been with the company, and say things like, "Wow" and "Awesome" as to laud their accomplishments.

You can even compliment them. You can mention that they are wearing a nice dress, or an awesome suit. It's called charm. Yes, flattery will get you everywhere.

I do all of these things in every interview.

When you walk out of that interview room, you want them to remember who you are!!

During the interview, show class and by all means, stay away from profanity. Yes!! I have had some candidates use profanity on an interview. I didn't hire them.

A lot of corporate interviews are structured, which means that they are going to ask each candidate the exact same questions, so how you answer them could determine whether you get the job or not.

And you must realize that there aren't really any wrong or right answers, but rather the best answers.

In the car business, if you are applying for a sales position, most of these interviews are not structured, as well as a lot of other professions.

For the interviewer, it's just a feel we get from the person we are interviewing as to whether or not we think that person can get the job done, but yet still, the responses they give, carry a lot of weight.

I would have to say that the single biggest mistake that candidates make is either not paying attention to the question that is being asked, or giving a response that has nothing to do with the question that was asked, or just simply talking too damn much.

When on an interview, be a good listener. Understand what the person is asking you and respond accordingly. Again, there normally isn't a right or wrong answer, but the most correct answer is what we, the interviewer, is looking for.

When you're asked, "What would make you a good leader?" Don't just say, "Well my department that I managed always performed well." ----- This should already be on your resume, so they already know that.

Instead, tell them why you are a good leader. "I feel that I am a good leader because I lead by example with my work ethic, being punctual and always professional. I never ask my team to do anything that I am not willing to do myself, and I always treat my staff with respect. I believe in chastising/counseling in private, and praising in public. These are just a few of the attributes that makes me a good leader."

Here is a question that a lot of people don't know how to answer.

"What would you say are your three weaknesses?"

The average person would say, "Well, I have a tendency to be late sometimes." or "I get distracted easily."

LOL ….. Well I can tell you that these things won't get you hired with me, because I don't deal with someone being late for work constantly or gets easily distracted.

NO!! – This is not what the interviewer wants to hear!!

You want to turn it around and use your strengths as weaknesses, as displayed here.

"I fell that my weaknesses are, that I am sometimes hard on myself, because I care about how I perform and if not performing well, I get down on myself at times."

During the interview, try not to think too hard about the question being asked, and if you do have to put more thought into it, then simply ask the interviewer, "Can we please come back to that question?"

Not everyone can do it, but if you can, try to answer the question as quickly as possible, and with confidence.

You must understand that the person who is conducting the interview is not trying to stump or trick you. They are simply looking for the best answers to their questions, and which candidate interviewed the best.

Please realize that every person being interviewed is reasonably qualified to fill the position for which you are applying, but it's the person that interviews the best and looks the best, who is going to get the job.

It's a combination of things. Out of everyone who was interviewed, who was the most professional, who interviewed the best, and who was the most likable.

If you nail all of these categories, then more than likely, you are going to get the job.

You could have been the most qualified, but didn't land the job because you didn't meet all of the criteria mentioned above.

Yes, you can be the most qualified individual, have the most degrees, graduated top of your class, etc, etc, etc, but if you can't master the art of the interview, you may very well find yourself unemployed, as a lot of college graduates do.

A college degree is nice to have. I wish I had one myself, but don't let not having a college degree deter you from achieving greatness.

It's what's in the heart and will of a person that determines their success, and not necessarily a piece of paper. Sure, a degree helps...... but without heart, will, determination, faith, and perseverance, that degree doesn't mean a thing.

THE RESUME

So you got the interview, but the reason you got the interview was probably because of your resume.

There are different resume formats, but regardless of the format, a resume should stand out.

Of course if you're a college graduate, you may not have much of a resume, but that's okay.

You still want to list your jobs, with the employer's name, your title/occupation, and dates worked (month/year)

The resume should be on quality paper (not typewriting or copier paper), but instead a thick grade of paper, which you should be able to get at any office supply store.

I would suggest an off white or beige color to make it stand out more, instead of a traditional white.

Atop your resume' should be your name, address, cell number and email address (This should all be in bold print)

Next line (First line) –should be your objective such as

Objective: - "Highly trained and motivated sales professional seeks employment with a progressive employer with the opportunity for advancement"

Next line should be your education and achievements

Education: Old Dominion University – B.S. in Business Administration – Summa Cum Laude – 3.89 GPA

There is no need to put the year you graduated as this will help the interviewer discern just how old you are, however, I am mainly talking about people who have been in the work force for at least ten years or longer. For those of you who have recently graduated college, it's okay to put your graduate year on the resume'.

Next is your job history. It should start from most recent and work backwards, and not the other way around.

Yes, I have seen resumes where the applicants have put their oldest job first. No!! It is always your most recent job and working back from there.

Work History: Sales Associate - Jumping Jack Trampolines – August 2016 – Present

- Salesperson of the month nine times during my employment
- Sold a record $12,600 in trampoline equipment in July of 2018
- Top sales rep in reference to referrals bought in
- Noted for my customer service and follow-up skills

As you can see, under work history, I just listed some highlights (bullet points) of my job and my accomplishments.

Of course, everyone, in fact most people, may not have any accomplishments to list, but that's okay. Just list your job responsibilities and what your job entailed. Limit you bullet points to five or six, unless you feel it necessary to list more.

The key is having a well-constructed resume that catches the eye of the employer.

Anyway, continue with your work history until you finish.

Ideally, you would want your resume to be one page, but two should be the absolute maximum.

If you have had a lot of jobs, you may want to try and condense your resume to keep it no longer than two pages.

At the end of your resume, you want to put at least two references with full names and phone numbers of the references.

And then put –

Additional References Available upon request

And that's it –

Indeed has made it easy to post your resume as all of them are formatted the same way, but you still want to have a quality resume in hand when they call you in for an interview.

Be prepared to hand it to the person interviewing you.

KEEPING THE JOB

So, you've applied for the job, interviewed for the job, and got the job!! Congrats!!!!!

Now you want to keep the job, right? Right!!!

Punctuality!!

I can't tell you how important this is and what an impression it makes on an employer.

For an employee to show up every day, without exception, without fail, and on time, is one of the best attributes an employee can have.

I have been working for 36 years and have been late a total of maybe ten times. I simply don't believe in being late for work.

Honesty. Always be honest and tell the truth. Follow the rules, no matter how silly or stupid you think they may be. They are in place for a reason, so adhere to them.

Next, be like a chameleon. Learn how to adjust to any environment. That has also been one of my gifts. You could throw me into any work environment with any group of people, regardless of race, temperaments, etc, and I will adjust and be able to get along with anyone.

Stay in your lane. Don't be concerned about what everyone else is doing, unless you're their manager or supervisor. Concentrate on your job and the task at hand.

Don't worry about who's coming in late, who took an extended lunch, who didn't do this and who didn't do that, and who left early. Just concentrate on you and get the job done. Don't worry about everyone else.

Be a team player. If you see someone struggling to complete a task, then offer help. Or if they ask you for help, go ahead and assist them. Being a team player and willing to help others shows leadership and compassion.

Stay late if you have to in order to complete a job if you're in a salaried position. Do whatever it takes to get the job done. It may not seem like it now, but your efforts will eventually get rewarded with a pay raise or promotion.

If you are an hourly worker, your employer may not grant or approve overtime, but if you think that you need to put in more time to get the job done, then put in an extra fifteen to thirty minutes to make it happen, and just like the salaried employee, you too will eventually see the fruits of your labor. It will eventually pay off in the long run for you.

Take pride in your work station and in your work. If you are required to write, then take pride in your penmanship. Practice your penmanship until it looks neat and is legible. Take pride in everything that you do and keep your work station neat and clean.

Avoid calling out. An employer wants an employee that is reliable, dependable and therefore someone who can be counted on, day in and day out.

Just because you have sick days, it doesn't mean that you have to use them.

Don't get me wrong, if you're really sick, then stay at home, but don't just be calling out of work for the heck of it.

In thirty six years, I have called out of work sick just once. I simply don't believe in it, or do it.

Be that tireless, devoted, dedicated, punctual, hard-working employee, and you will never have a problem keeping a job.

Well, that's my time peeps.

I hope this book has helped you as that was its intent.

Everything I have included in this book, I have lived, breathed, and experienced, and have made a lot of money because of it, and you will too!!

Good luck in all current and future endeavors!!!

May God bless you!!

Printed in the United States
By Bookmasters